Impressum
Verlag: BABADADA GmbH, Nedderfeld 112 , 22529 Hamburg
Geschäftsführer / Verlagsleitung: Harald Hof
Druck: Books on Demand GmbH, In de Tarpen 42, 22848 Norderstedt

Imprint
Publisher: BABADADA GmbH, Nedderfeld 112 , 22529 Hamburg, Germany
Managing Director / Publishing direction: Harald Hof
Print: Books on Demand GmbH, In de Tarpen 42, 22848 Norderstedt

lekol

school

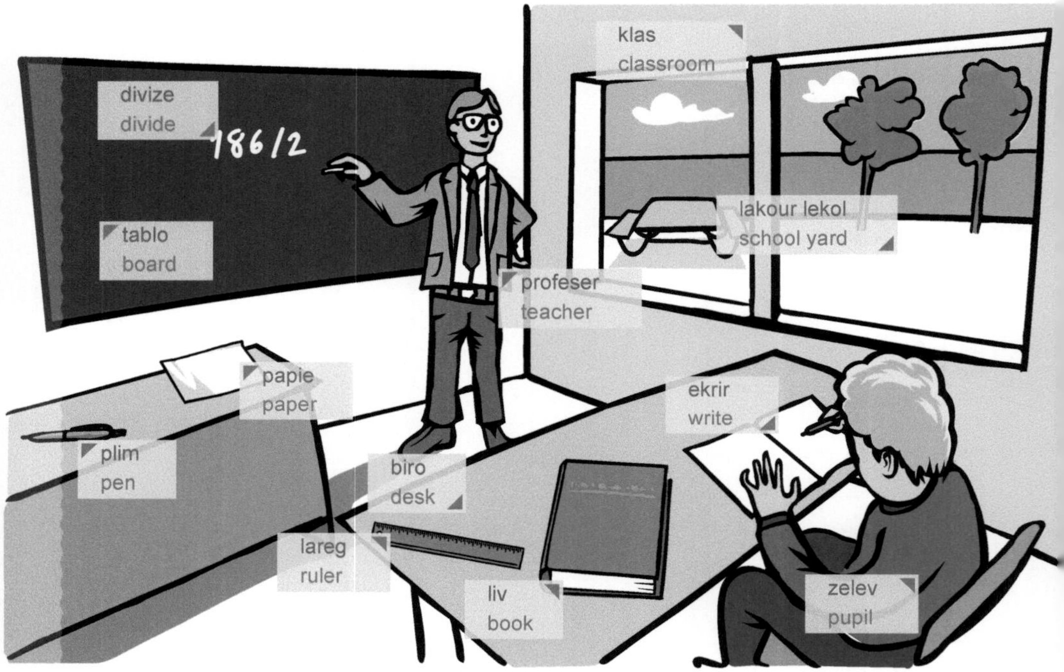
klas
classroom
divize
divide
186/2
tablo
board
lakour lekol
school yard
profeser
teacher
papie
paper
ekrir
write
plim
pen
biro
desk
lareg
ruler
liv
book
zelev
pupil

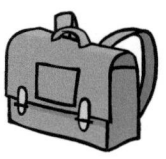

sak lekol

satchel

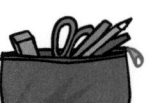

plimie

pencil case

kreyon

pencil

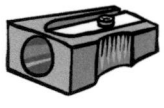

egizwar

pencil sharpener

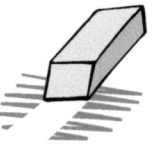

gom

rubber

kaye desin

drawing pad

desin

drawing

pinso

paintbrush

bwat lapintir

paint box

sizo

scissors

lakol

glue

kaye devwar

exercise book

devwar

homework

nimero

number

azoute

add

retire

subtract

miltipliye

multiply

kalkile

calculate

let

letter

alfabet

alphabet

mo

word

text
text

lir
read

lakre
chalk

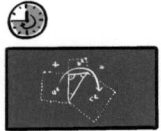

leson
lesson

rezis
register

lexame
exam

sertifika
certificate

iniform lekol
school uniform

ledikasion
education

lansiklopedi
encyclopedia

liniversite
university

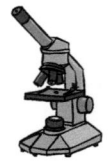

mikroskop
microscope

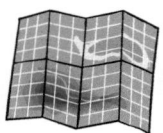

map
map

poubel
waste-paper basket

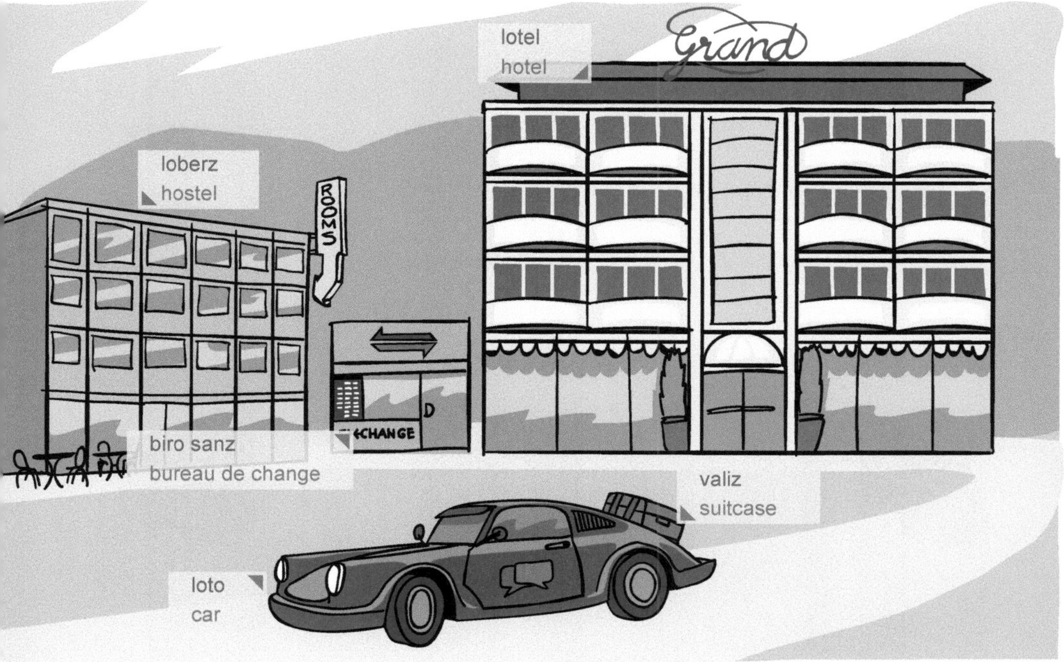

lotel
hotel
Grand
loberz
hostel
ROOMS
biro sanz
bureau de change
valiz
suitcase
loto
car

langaz
language

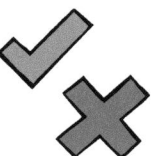

wi / non
yes / no

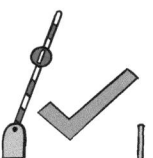

okay
Okay

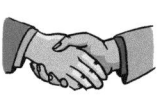

Alo
hello

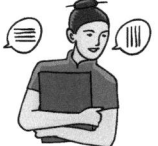

tradikter
translator

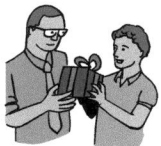

Mersi
Thank you

komie sa..?

how much is…?

Mo pa pe konpran

I do not understand

problem

problem

Bonswar!

Good evening!

Bonzour!

Good morning!

Bonn nwi!

Good night!

o-revwar

bye bye

direksion

direction

bagaz

luggage

sak

bag

sak-a-do

backpack

ot

guest

pies

room

sak kousaz

sleeping bag

latant

tent

lofis tourism

tourist information

laplaz

beach

kart kredi

credit card

ti-dezene

breakfast

dezene

lunch

dine

dinner

biye

ticket

lasanser

lift

tem

stamp

frontier

border

ladwann

customs

lanbasad

embassy

viza

visa

paspor

passport

transpor
transport

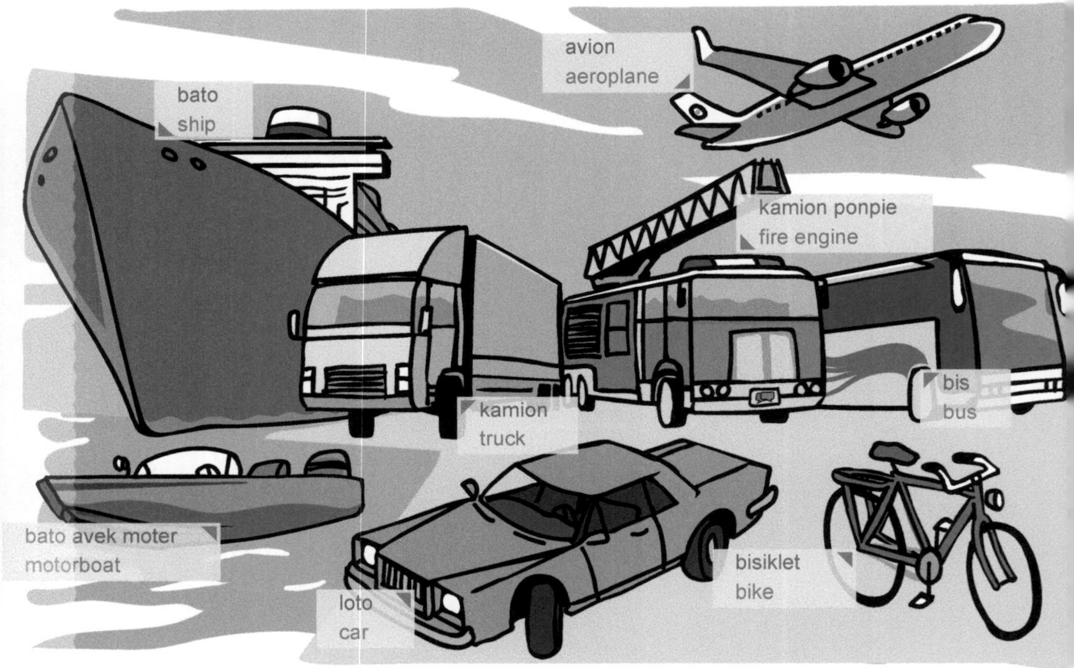

avion
aeroplane

bato
ship

kamion ponpie
fire engine

kamion
truck

bis
bus

bato avek moter
motorboat

loto
car

bisiklet
bike

feri

ferry

bato

boat

motosiklet

motorbike

loto lapolis

police car

loto lekours

racing car

loto lokasion

rental car

ko-vwatiraz

car sharing

kamion towing

breakdown truck

kamion salte

refuse truck

moter

motor

lesans

fuel

filing

petrol station

pano indikasion

traffic sign

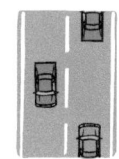

trafik

traffic

anbouteyaz

traffic jam

parking

car park

stasion trin

train station

ray

tracks

trin

train

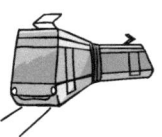

tram

tram

vagon

carriage

transpor - transport

elikopter

helicopter

aeropor

airport

towing

tower

pasaze

passenger

kontener

container

karton

carton

sario

cart

panie

basket

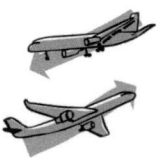

dekole / aterir

take off / land

lavil
city

vilaz

village

sant-vil

city centre

lakaz

house

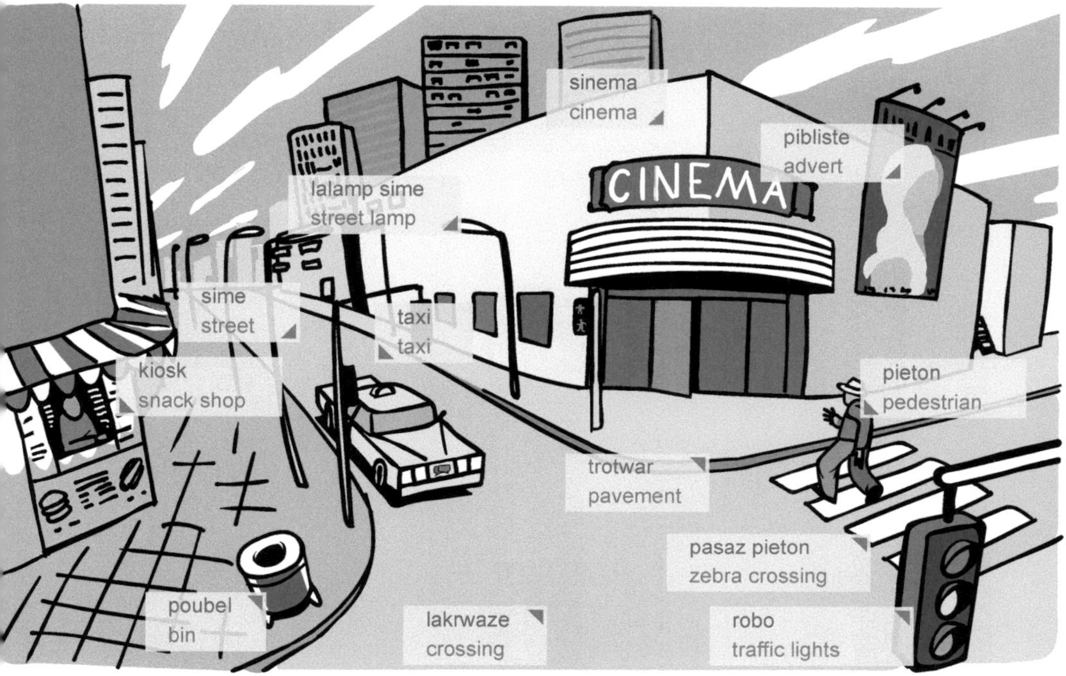
sinema
cinema
CINEMA
pibliste
advert
lalamp sime
street lamp
sime
street
taxi
taxi
kiosk
snack shop
pieton
pedestrian
trotwar
pavement
pasaz pieton
zebra crossing
poubel
bin
lakrwaze
crossing
robo
traffic lights

kabann

hut

flat

flat

stasion trin

train station

minisipalite

town hall

MUSEUM

mize

museum

lekol

school

liniversite

university

labank

bank

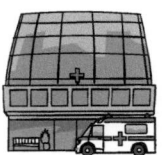

lopital

hospital

lotel

hotel

farmasi

pharmacy

biro

office

libreri

book shop

magazin

shop

fleris

florist's

sipermarse

supermarket

bazar

market

gran magazin

department store

pwasonnri

fishmonger's

sant komersial

shopping centre

lepor

harbour

park
park

labank
bench

pon
bridge

leskalie
stairs

metro
underground

tinel
tunnel

bistop
bus stop

bar
bar

restoran
restaurant

bwat-a-let
postbox

pano
street sign

parkmet
parking meter

zoo
zoo

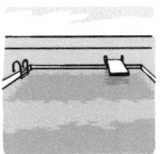

pisinn
swimming pool

moske
mosque

laferm
farm

polision
pollution

simitier
graveyard

legliz
church

lespas pou zwe
playground

tanp
temple

peizaz
landscape

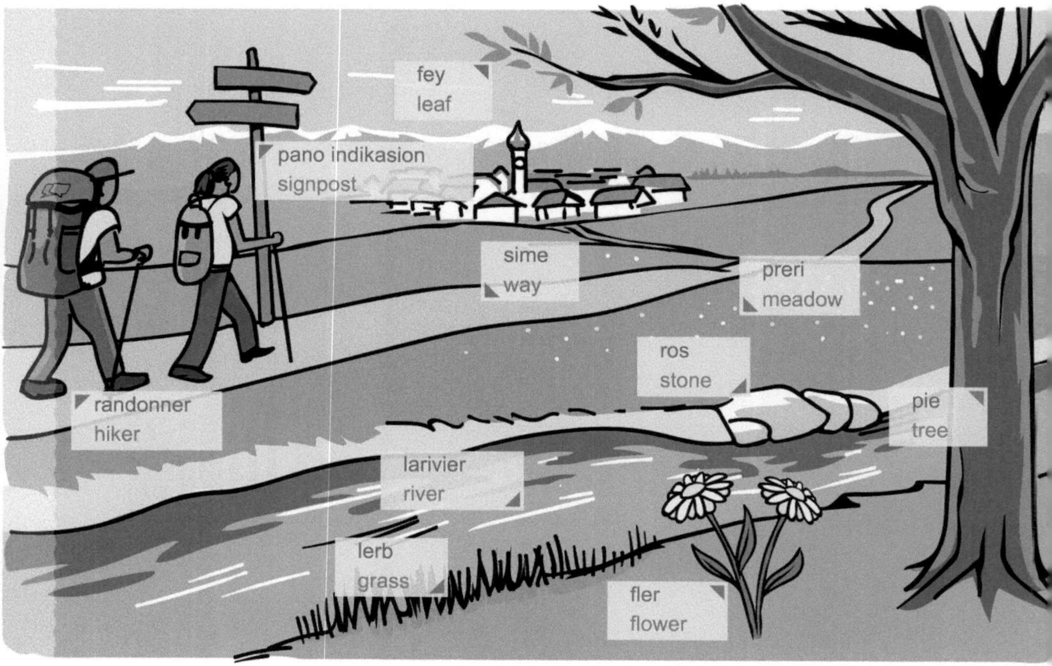

fey
leaf

pano indikasion
signpost

sime
way

preri
meadow

ros
stone

randonner
hiker

pie
tree

larivier
river

lerb
grass

fler
flower

lavale

valley

kolinn

hill

lak

lake

bwa

forest

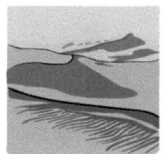

dezer

desert

volkan

volcano

sato

castle

larkansiel

rainbow

sanpinion

mushroom

palmie

palm tree

moutik

mosquito

mous

fly

fourmi

ant

abey

bee

zarenie

spider

koksinel
beetle

grenouy
frog

ekirey
squirrel

erison
hedgehog

lapin
hare

ibou
owl

zwazo
bird

sign
swan

sangliye
boar

serf
deer

elan
moose

dam
dam

eolienn
wind turbine

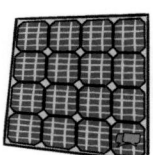

pano soler
solar panel

klima
climate

restoran

restaurant

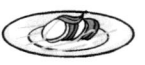

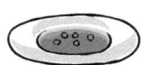

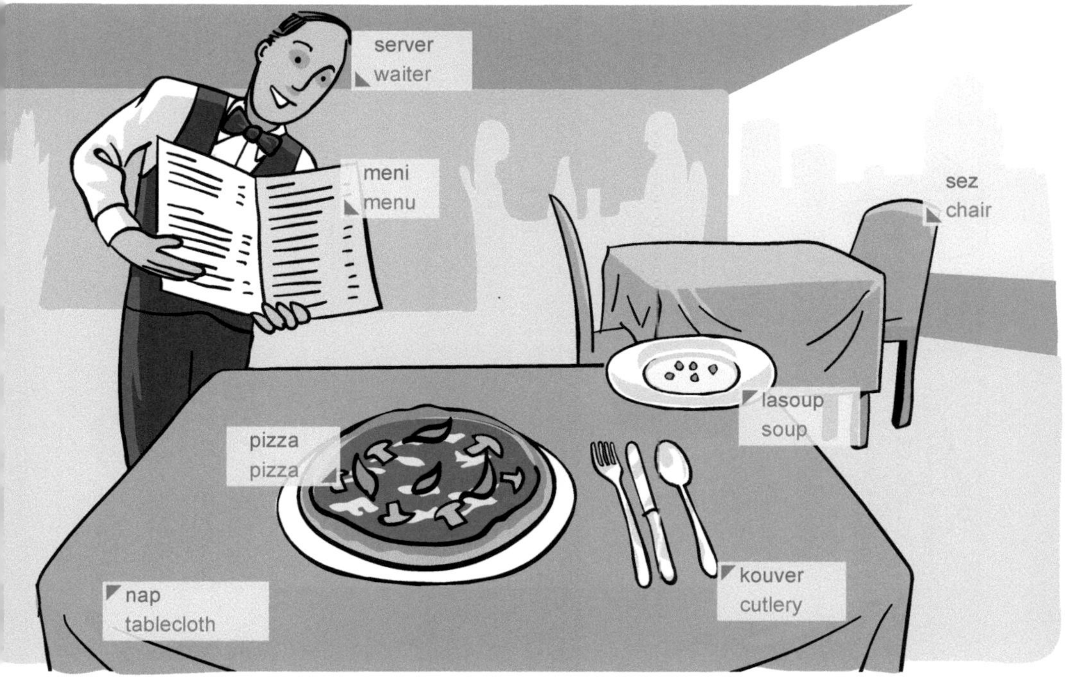

server
waiter
meni
menu
sez
chair
lasoup
soup
pizza
pizza
kouver
cutlery
nap
tablecloth

lantre
starter

pla prinsipal
main course

deser
dessert

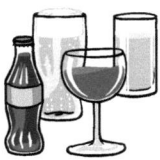

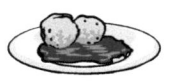

labwason
drinks

manze
food

boutey
bottle

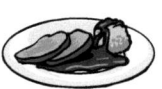

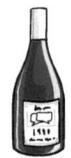

fast food
....
fast food

take-away
....
street food

teyer
....
teapot

po disik
....
sugar bowl

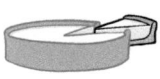

porsion
....
portion

masinn expresso
....
espresso machine

sez-ot
....
high chair

bill
....
bill

plato
....
tray

kouto
....
knife

fourset
....
fork

kwiyer
....
spoon

ti-kwiyer
....
teaspoon

serviet
....
serviette

ver
....
glass

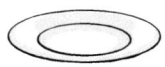

lasiet

plate

lasiet

soup plate

soukoup

saucer

lasos

sauce

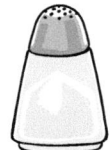

po disel

salt pot

moulin dipwav

pepper mill

vineg

vinegar

delwil

oil

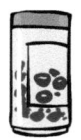

zepis

spices

ketchup

ketchup

lamoutard

mustard

mayonez

mayonnaise

sipermarse
supermarket

promosion
special offer
FOR
klian
customer
prodwi a baz dile
dairy
frwi
fruit
trole
trolley

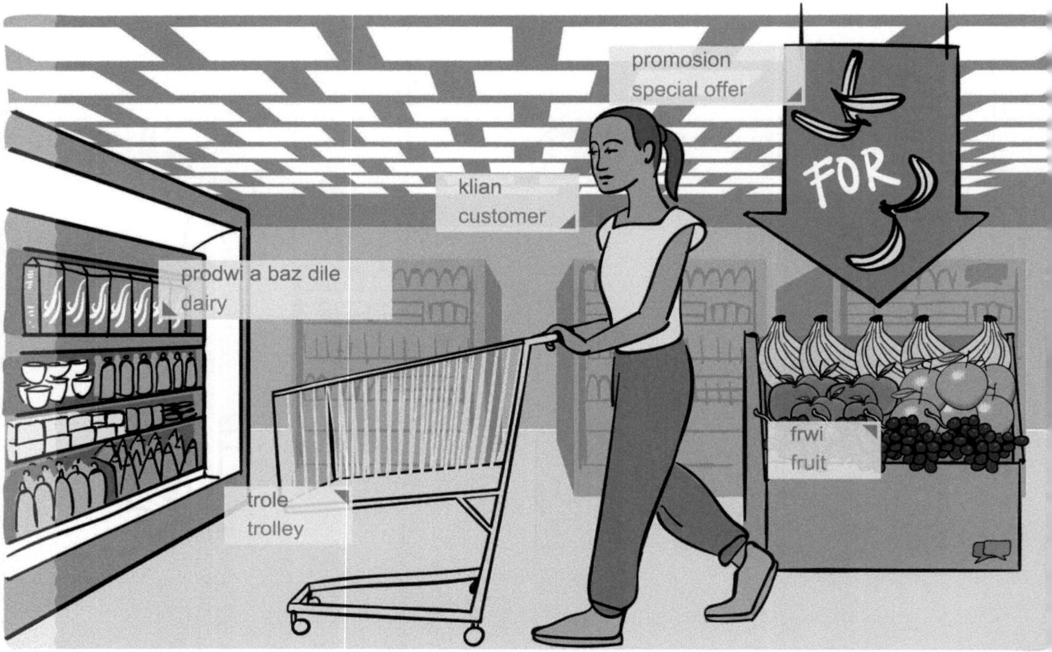

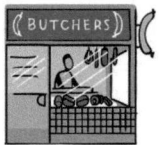

BUTCHERS

bousri

butcher´s

BAKERY

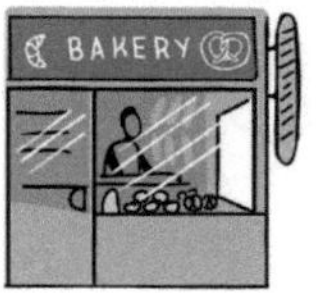

boulanzri

baker´s

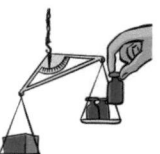

peze

weigh

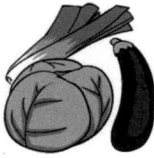

legim

vegetables

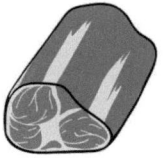

laviann

meat

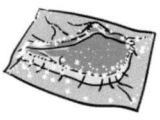

aliman konzele

frozen food

sarkitri

cold meat

bwat konserv

tinned food

lapoud masinn

washing powder

bonbon

sweets

komision

household products

deterzan

cleaning products

vandez

salesperson

lakes

till

kesie

cashier

lalis komision

shopping list

ouvertir

opening hours

portfey

wallet

kart kredi

credit card

sak

bag

sak plastik

plastic bag

delo

water

zi

juice

dile

milk

coca

coke

divin

wine

labier

beer

lalkol

alcohol

sokola so

cocoa

dite

tea

kafe

coffee

expresso

espresso

cappuccino

cappuccino

banann

banana

pom

apple

zoranz

orange

melon

melon

sitron

lemon

karot

carrot

lay

garlic

banbou

bamboo

zwayon

onion

sanpiyon

mushroom

nwazet

nuts

minn

noodles

spageti

spaghetti

diri

rice

salad

salad

chips

chips

pomdeter frir

fried potatoes

pizza

pizza

burger

hamburger

sandwich

sandwich

eskalop

cutlet

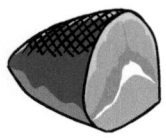

zanbon

ham

salami

salami

sosis

sausage

poul

chicken

roti

roast

pwason

fish

oatmeal
porridge oats

muesli
muesli

kornbif
cornflakes

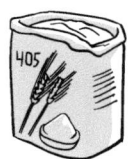

lafarinn
flour

krwasan
croissant

ti-dipin
bread roll

dipin
bread

dipin griye
toast

biskwi
biscuits

diber
butter

fromaz blan
curd

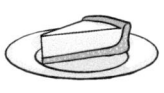

gato
cake

dizef
egg

dizef frir
fried egg

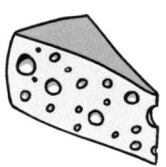

fromaz
cheese

sorbe

ice cream

disik

sugar

dimiel

honey

konfitir

jam

nouga

chocolate spread

kari

curry

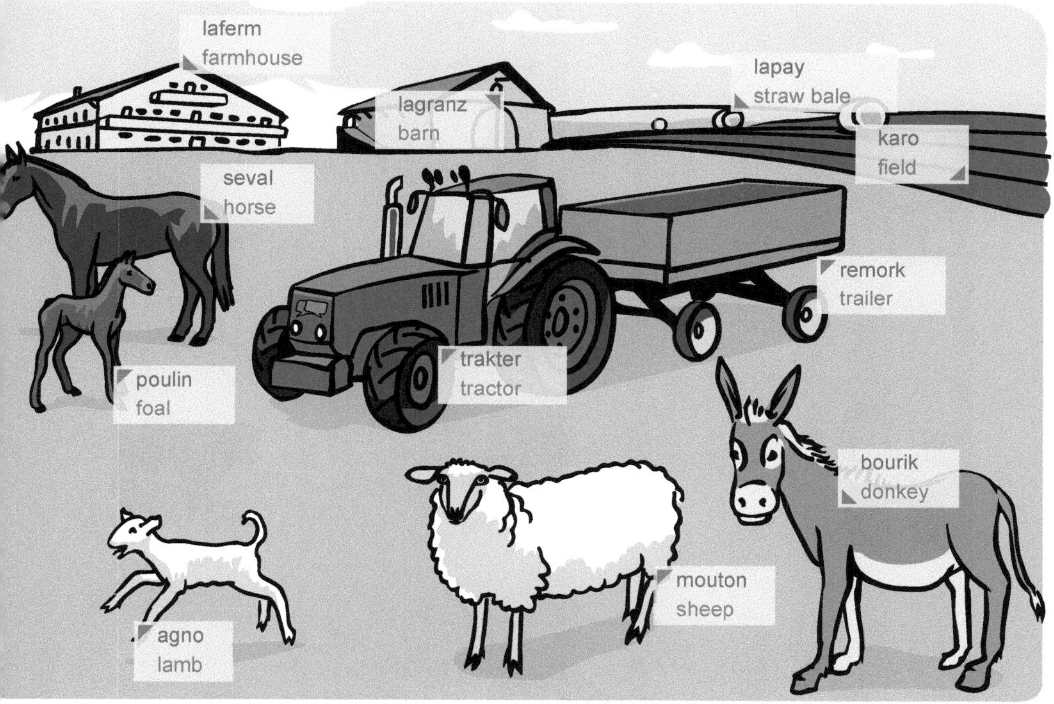

laferm
farmhouse

lapay
straw bale

lagranz
barn

karo
field

seval
horse

remork
trailer

poulin
foal

trakter
tractor

bourik
donkey

mouton
sheep

agno
lamb

kabri
goat

vas
cow

vo
calf

koson
pig

ti-koson
piglet

toro
bull

lezwa

goose

kanar

duck

pousin

chick

poul

hen

kok

cock

lera

rat

sat

cat

souri

mouse

bef

ox

lisien

dog

lakaz lisien

doghouse

tiyo

garden hose

arozwar

watering can

laserp

scythe

saret

plough

fosi

sickle

pios

hoe

fours

pitchfork

lars

axe

bouret

wheelbarrow

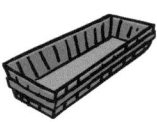

kiv

trough

bwat dile

milk can

sak

sack

fencing

fence

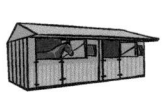

letab

stable

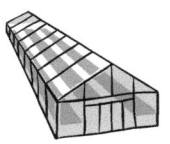

laser

greenhouse

later

soil

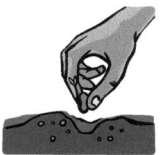

lagrin

seed

langre

fertilizer

masinn pou fer rekolt

combine harvester

laferm - farm

rekolte

harvest

rekolt

harvest

ignam

yams

dible

wheat

soya

soy

pomdeter

potato

may

corn

colza

rapeseed

zarb frwitie

fruit tree

maniok

cassava

sereal

cereals

lakaz
house

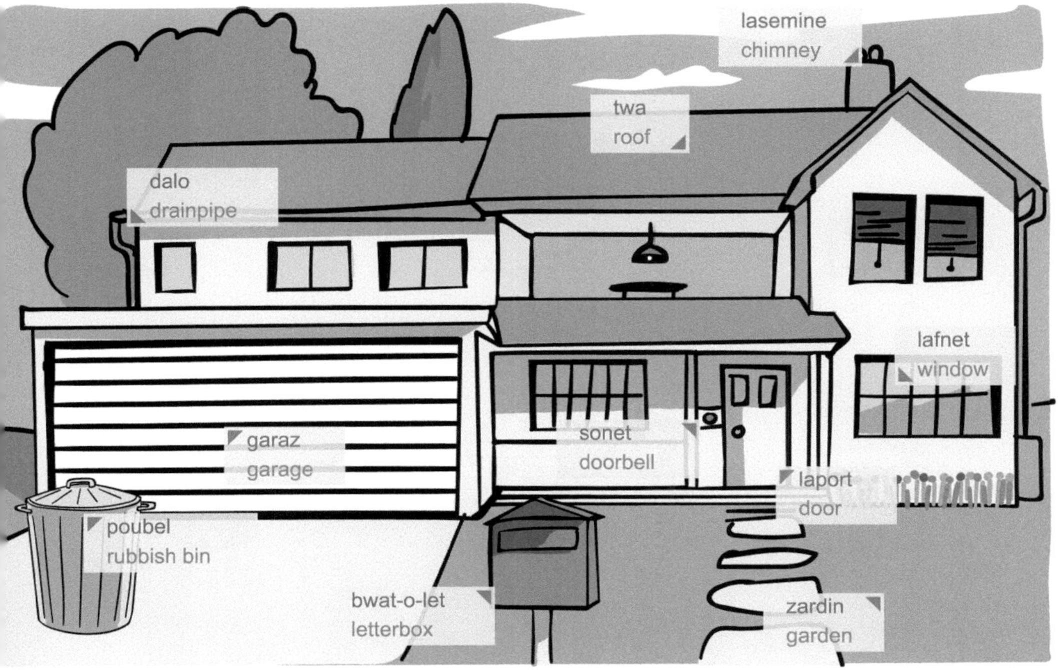
lasemine
chimney
twa
roof
dalo
drainpipe
lafnet
window
garaz
garage
sonet
doorbell
laport
door
poubel
rubbish bin
bwat-o-let
letterbox
zardin
garden

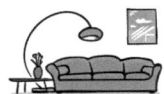

salon

living room

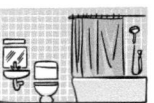

saldebin

bathroom

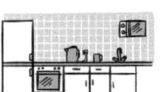

lakwizinn

kitchen

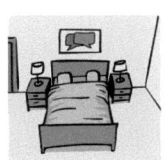

lasam

bedroom

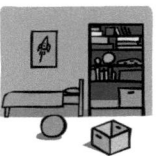

lasam zanfan

child's room

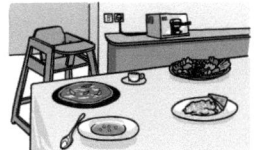

salamanze

dining room

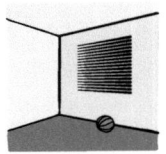

sali

floor

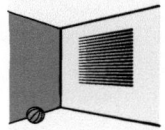

miray

wall

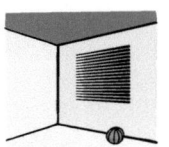

plafon

ceiling

lakav

cellar

sona

sauna

balkon

balcony

teras

terrace

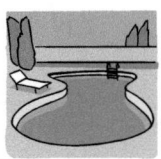

pisinn

pool

masinn koup gazon

lawn mower

dra

sheet

kwet

bedspread

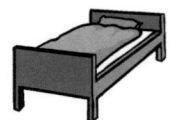

lili

bed

balie

broom

seo

bucket

take lalimier

switch

salon

living room

papie-pin
wallpaper
foto
picture
lalamp
lamp
letazer
shelf
larmwar
cupboard
televizion
television
lasemine
fireplace
fler
flower
kousin
cushion
sofa
sofa
vaz
vase
rimot-kontrol
remote control

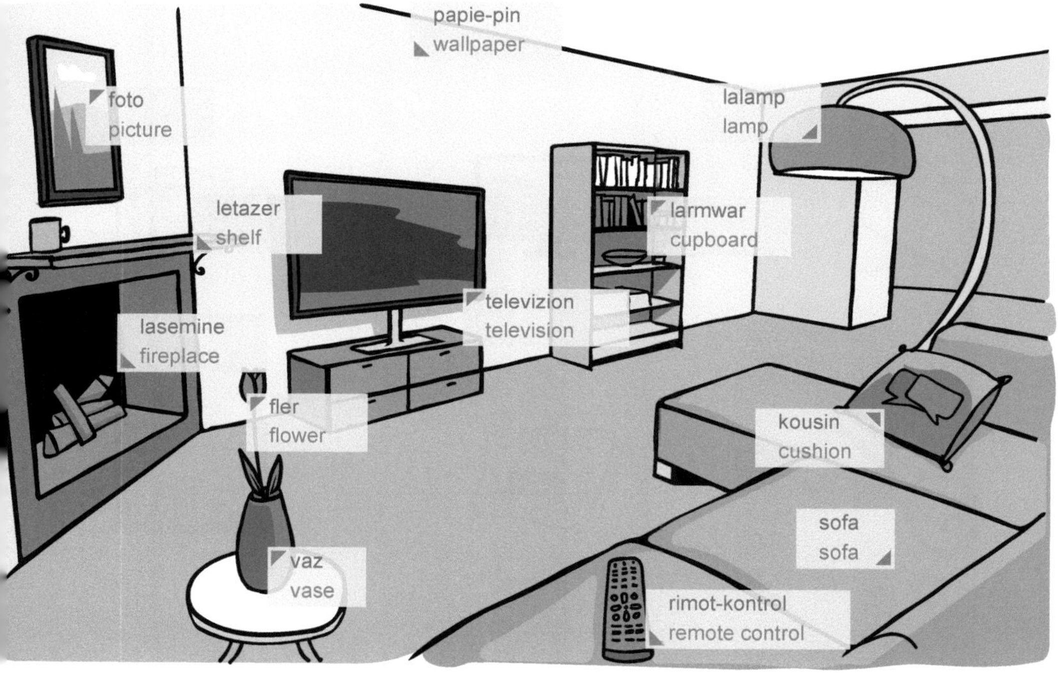

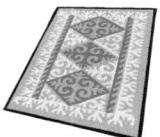

tapi

carpet

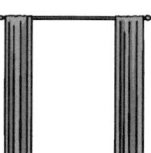

rido

curtain

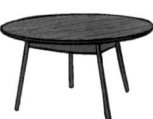

latab

table

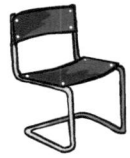

sez

chair

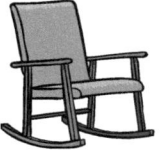

rocking chair

rocking chair

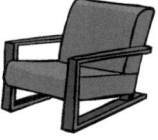

fotey

armchair

liv

book

kouvertir

blanket

dekorasion

decoration

dibwa foye

firewood

fim

film

hi-fi

hi-fi equipment

lakle

key

zournal

newspaper

lapintir

painting

poster

poster

radio

radio

bloknot

notepad

laspirater

hoover

kaktis

cactus

labouzi

candle

salon - living room

lakwizinn
kitchen

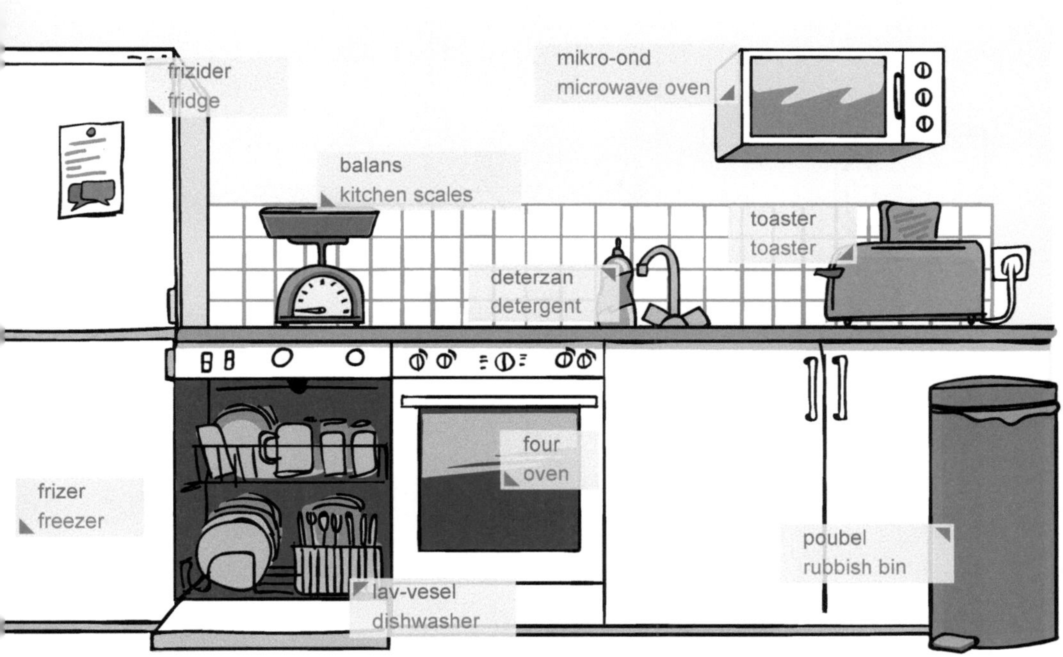

frizider
fridge
mikro-ond
microwave oven
balans
kitchen scales
toaster
toaster
deterzan
detergent
four
oven
frizer
freezer
poubel
rubbish bin
lav-vesel
dishwasher

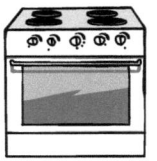

four
cooker

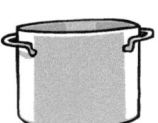

kasrol
pot

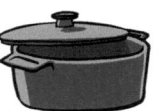

marmit
cast-iron pot

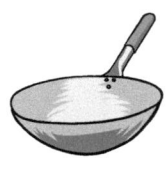

wok
wok / kadai

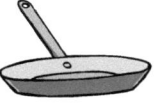

pwal
pan

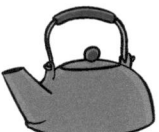

boulwar
kettle

steamer

steamer

plak kwison

baking tray

vesel

crockery

goble

mug

bol

bowl

baget sinwa

chopsticks

lous

ladle

spatil

spatula

fwet

whisk

paswar

strainer

tami

sieve

larap

grater

mortie

mortar

griyad

barbecue

lasemine

open fire

biyo

chopping board

roulo

rolling pin

tirbouson

corkscrew

bwat konserv

can

ouvbwat

can opener

legan proteksion

pot holder

lavabo

sink

bros

brush

leponz

sponge

blender

blender

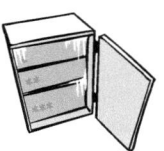

konzelater

deep freezer

bibron

baby bottle

robine

tap

saldebin
bathroom

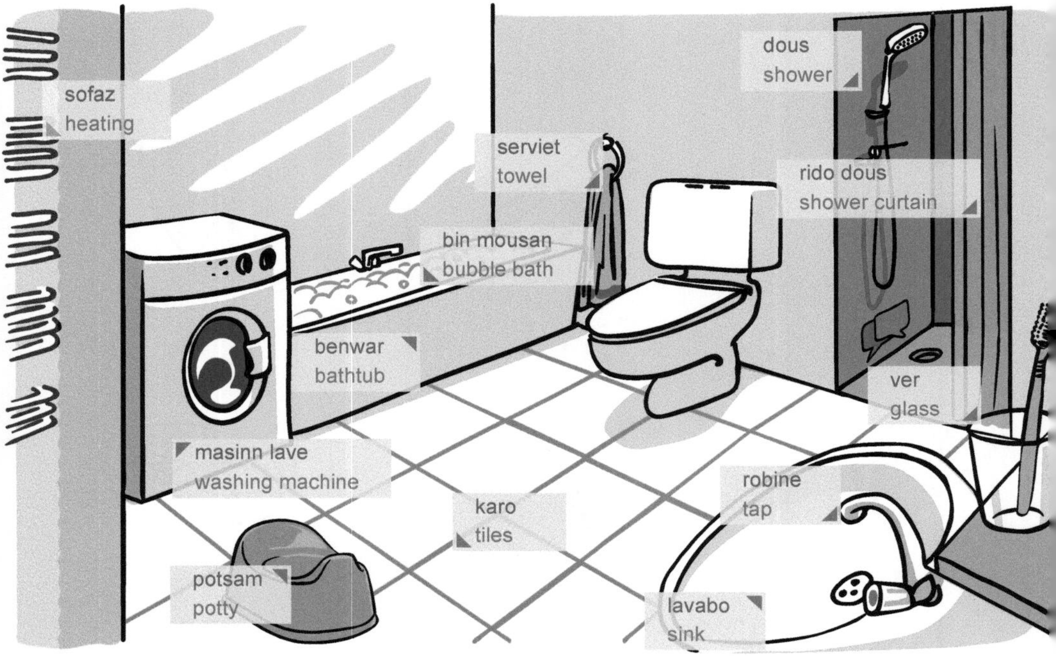

sofaz
heating
serviet
towel
dous
shower
rido dous
shower curtain
bin mousan
bubble bath
benwar
bathtub
masinn lave
washing machine
karo
tiles
potsam
potty
robine
tap
ver
glass
lavabo
sink

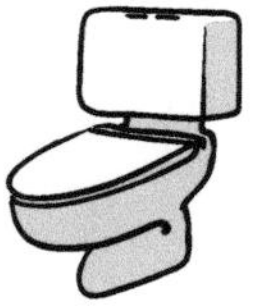

twalet
toilet

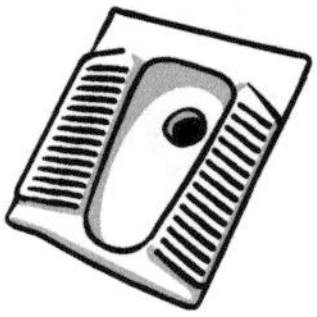

twalet
squat toilet

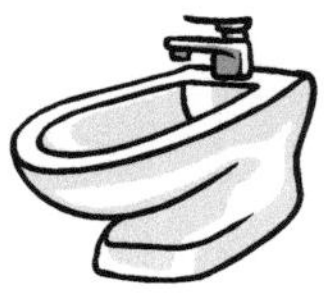

bide
bidet

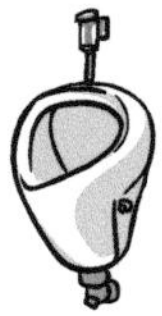

piswar
urinal

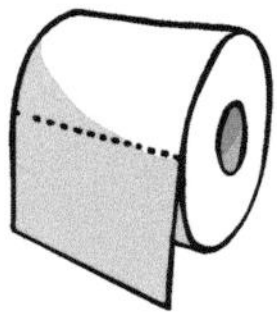

papie twalet
toilet paper

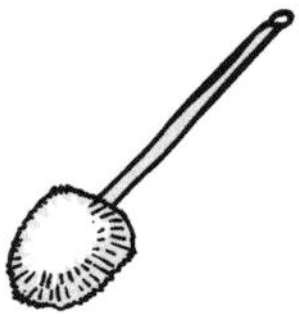

bros twalet
toilet brush

bros ledan

toothbrush

dantifris

toothpaste

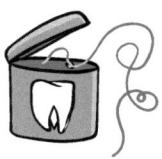

fil danter

dental floss

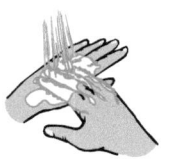

lave

wash

ti-bin

handheld shower

dous

douche

basin

basin

bros ledo

back brush

savon

soap

zel dous

shower gel

sanpwin

shampoo

gandebin

flannel

drin

drain

lakrem

cream

deodoran

deodorant

mirwar

mirror

mirwar

hand mirror

razwar

razor

lamous pou raze

shaving foam

apre-razaz

aftershave

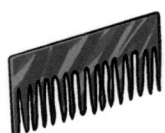

pengn

comb

bros

brush

seswar

hair dryer

lak

hairspray

makiyaz

makeup

dirouz

lipstick

verni

nail varnish

cotton wool

cotton wool

tay-zong

nail scissors

parfin

perfume

trous twalet

washbag

stoul

stool

balans

weighing scale

penwar

bathrobe

legan netwayaz

rubber gloves

tanpon

tampon

serviet izienik

sanitary towel

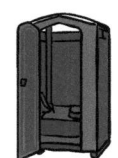

twalet simik

chemical toilet

lasam zanfan

child's room

revey
alarm clock
doudou
cuddly toy
ti loto
toy car
ose
rattle
lakaz zouzou
doll's house
kado
present

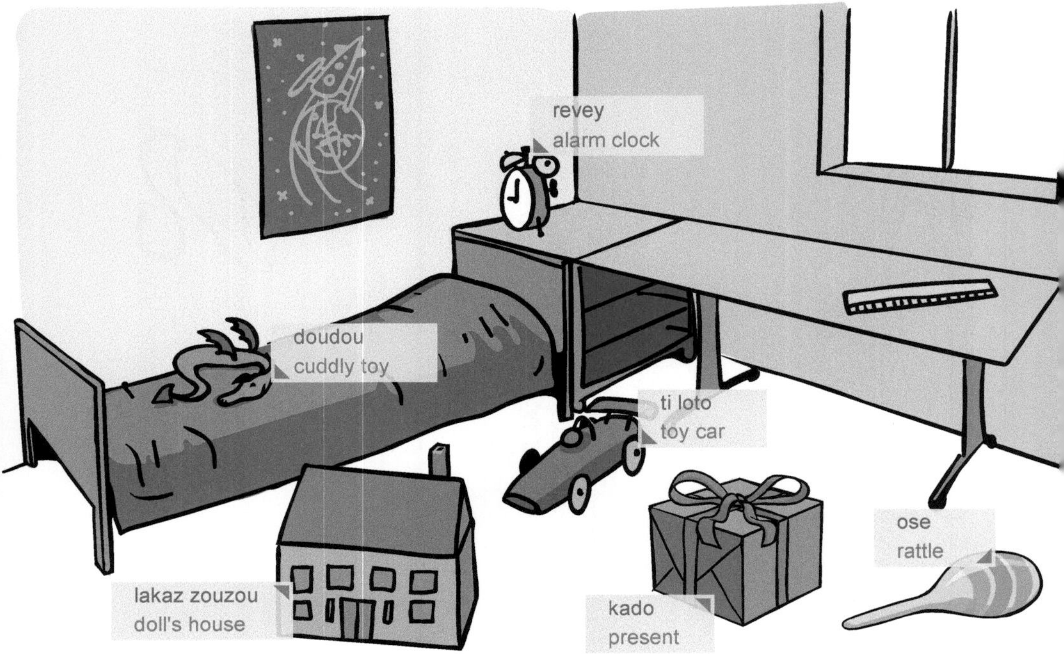

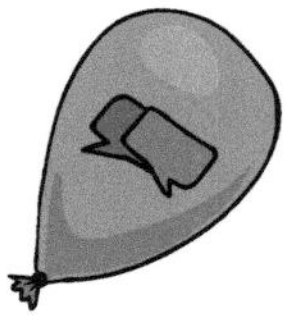

balon

balloon

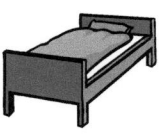

lili

bed

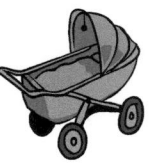

pouset

pram

kart

deck of cards

puzzle

jigsaw

SUPER
MEGA

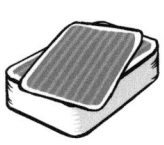

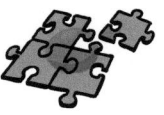

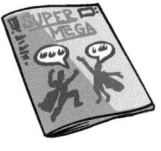

tikomik

comic

lego

lego bricks

lego

building blocks

figirinn

action figure

grenouyer

babygrow

frisbee

frisbee

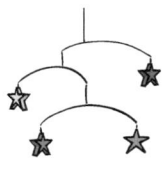

mobil

mobile

zwe

board game

lede

dice

trin zouzou

model train set

siset

dummy

fet

party

liv ek zimaz

picture book

boul

ball

poupet

doll

zwe

play

bak-a-sab
....
sandpit

balanswar
....
swing

zouzou
....
toys

game
....
video game console

trisik
....
tricycle

nounours
....
teddy bear

larmwar
....
wardrobe

linz
clothing

soset
....
socks

leba
....
stockings

kolan
....
tights

esarp
scarf

sintir
belt

parapli
umbrella

t-shirt
t-shirt

bot
boots

pantouf
slippers

tenis
trainers

sandalet
sandals

soulie
shoes

bot an karotsou
rubber boots

souvetman
underpants

soutiengorz
bra

vest
vest

body
body

pantalon
trousers

jeans
jeans

zip
skirt

blouz
blouse

simiz
shirt

pull-over
pullover

blouzon ek kapison
hoodie

vest
blazer

jaket
jacket

manto
coat

pardesi
raincoat

kostim
costume

rob
dress

rob lamarye
wedding dress

kostim

suit

robdesam

nightgown

pizama

pyjamas

sari

sari

foular

headscarf

tirban

turban

bourka

burqa

kaftan

kaftan

abaya

abaya

mayo de bin

swimsuit

mayo de bin

trunks

sorti de sekour

shorts

linz spor

tracksuit

tabliye

apron

legan

gloves

bouton

button

linet

glasses

brasle

bracelet

kolie

necklace

bag

ring

zanon

earring

bone

cap

sint

coat hanger

sapo

hat

kravat

tie

fermetirekler

zip

elmet

helmet

bretel

braces

iniform lekol

school uniform

iniform

uniform

bavwar
bib

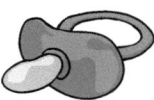

siset
dummy

lanz
nappy

biro
office

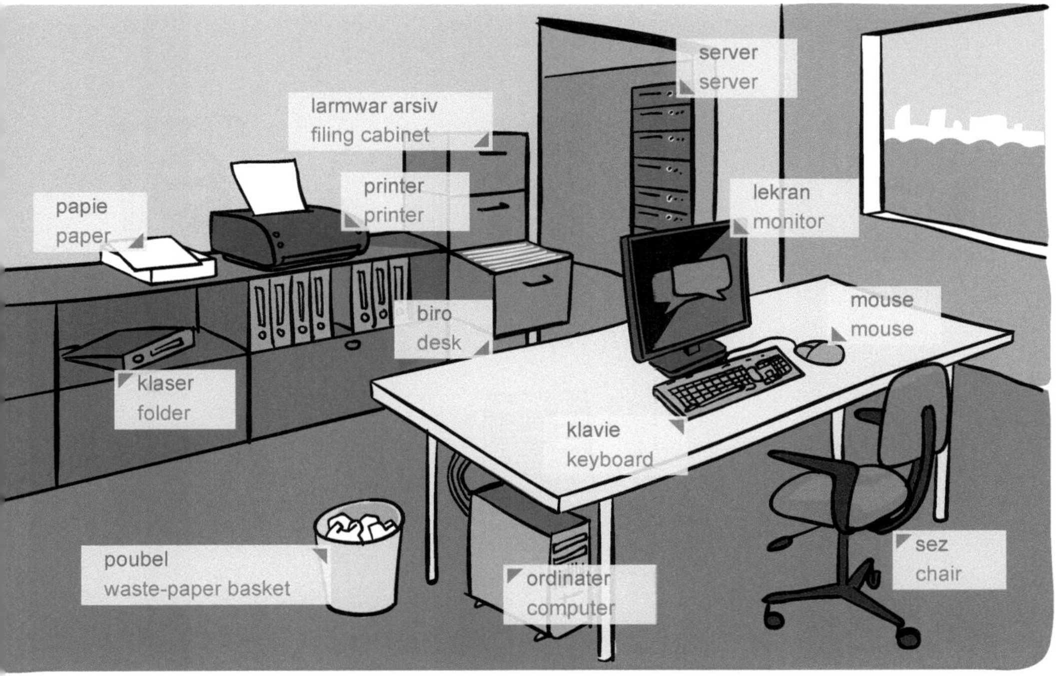

larmwar arsiv
filing cabinet

server
server

printer
printer

lekran
monitor

papie
paper

biro
desk

mouse
mouse

klaser
folder

klavie
keyboard

poubel
waste-paper basket

sez
chair

ordinater
computer

mug
coffee mug

kalkilatris
calculator

internet
internet

laptop
laptop

let
letter

mesaz
message

portab
mobile

rezo
network

fotokopi
photocopier

lozisiel
software

telefonn
telephone

priz
plug socket

fax
fax machine

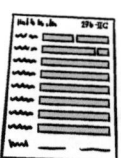

form
form

dokiman
document

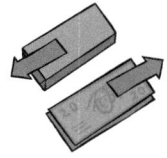

aste

buy

peye

pay

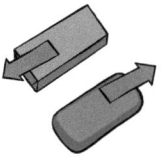

fer biznes

trade

larzan

money

USD

dolar

dollar

EUR

euro

euro

JPY

yen

yen

RUB

rouble

rouble

CHF

fran swis

Swiss franc

CNY

renminbi yuan

renminbi yuan

INR

roupi

rupee

distribiter biye

cashpoint

biro sanz

bureau de change

lor

gold

larzan

silver

petrol

oil

lenerzi

energy

pri

price

kontra

contract

tax

tax

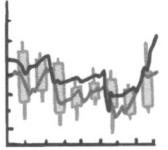

aksion

stock

travay

work

anplwaye

employee

anplwayer

employer

lizinn

factory

magazin

shop

polisie
police officer

ponpie
fireman

kwizinie
cook

dokter
doctor

pilot
pilot

zardinie

gardener

sarpantie

carpenter

koutirier

seamstress

ziz

judge

simis

chemist

akter

actor

sofer bis

bus driver

sofer taxi

taxi driver

peser

fisherman

bonn

cleaning lady

zouvriye twa lakaz

roofer

server

waiter

saser

hunter

pint

painter

boulanze

baker

elektrisien

electrician

zouvriye

builder

inzenier

engineer

bouse

butcher

plonbie

plumber

fakter

postman

solda

soldier

arsitek

architect

kesie

cashier

fleris

florist

kwafez

hairdresser

chek

conductor

mekanisien

mechanic

kapitenn

captain

dantis

dentist

siantis

scientist

rabi

rabbi

imam

imam

mwann

monk

pret

clergyman

zouti

tools

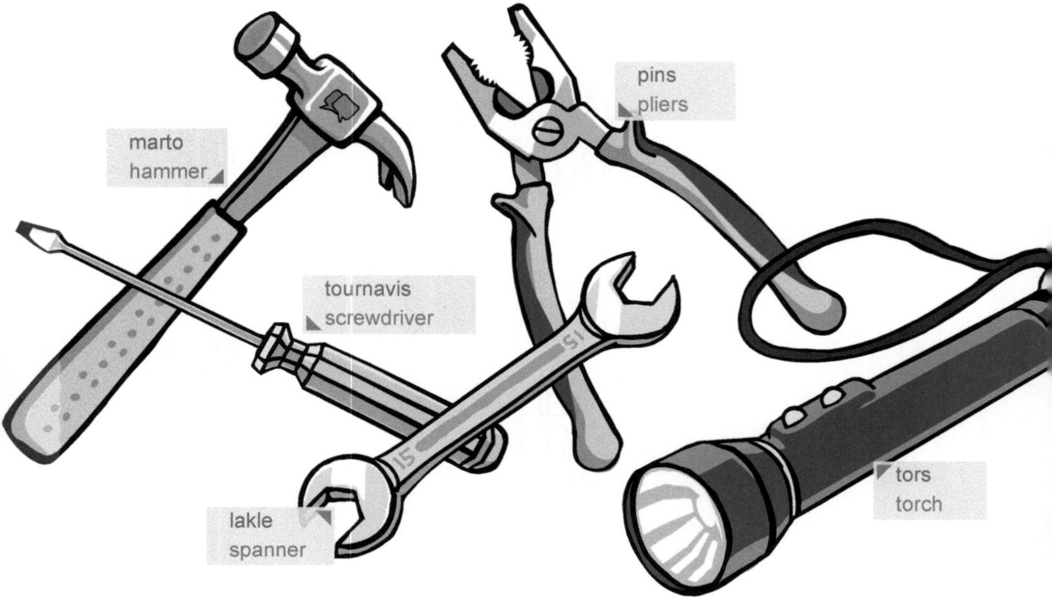
marto
hammer
pins
pliers
tournavis
screwdriver
lakle
spanner
tors
torch

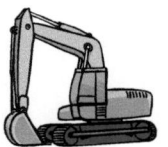

peltez

digger

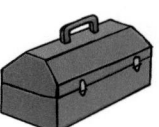

bwat zouti

toolbox

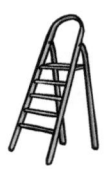

lesel

ladder

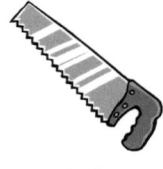

lasi

saw

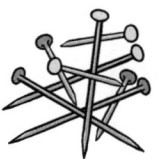

koulou

nails

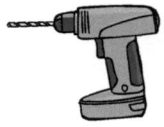

persez

drill

aranze
repair

lapel
shovel

Ayo!
Damn!

lapel
dustpan

po lapintir
paint pot

vis
screws

instriman lamizik
musical instruments

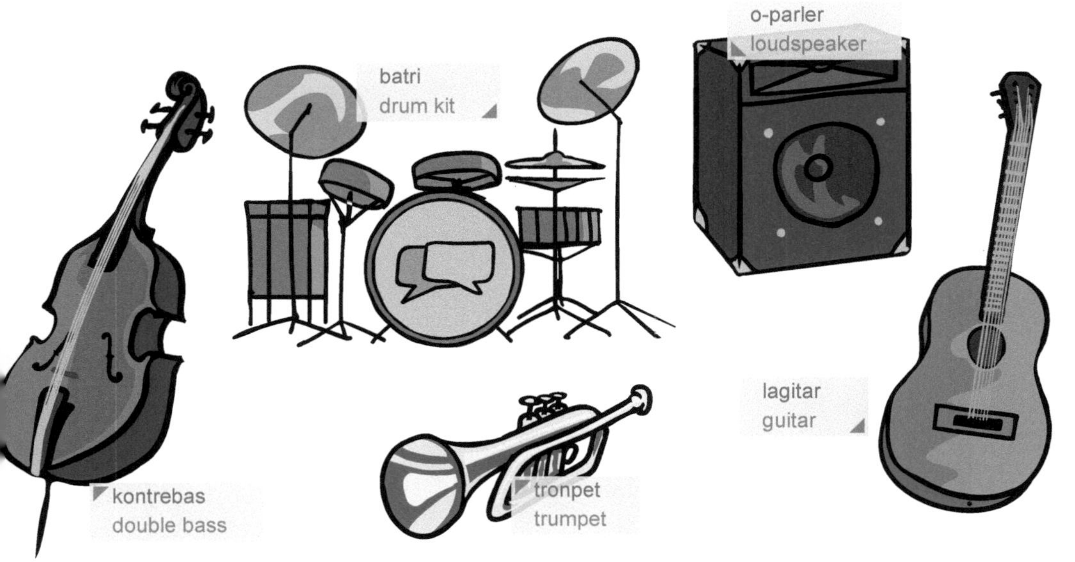

batri
drum kit

o-parler
loudspeaker

lagitar
guitar

kontrebas
double bass

tronpet
trumpet

piano
piano

violon
violin

bas
bass

tinbal
timpani

tanbour
drums

klavie
keyboard

saxofonn
saxophone

laflit
flute

mikro
microphone

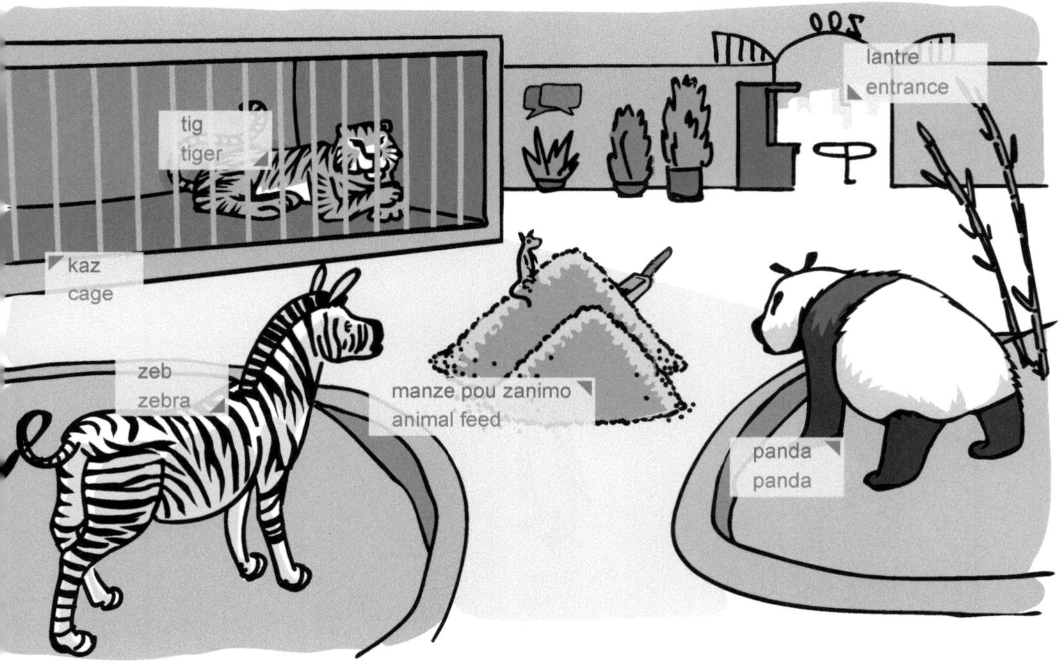

lantre
entrance

tig
tiger

kaz
cage

zeb
zebra

manze pou zanimo
animal feed

panda
panda

zanimo

animals

lelefan

elephant

kangourou

kangaroo

rinoceros

rhino

gori

gorilla

lours

bear

samo

camel

lotris

ostrich

lion

lion

zako

monkey

flaman roz

flamingo

peroke

parrot

lours poler

polar bear

pingwi

penguin

rekin

shark

pan

peacock

serpan

snake

krokodil

crocodile

gardien zoo

zookeeper

fok

seal

zagwar

jaguar

poney
pony

leopar
leopard

ipopotam
hippo

ziraf
giraffe

leg
eagle

sangliye
boar

pwason
fish

torti
turtle

mors
walrus

renar
fox

gazel
gazelle

foutborl ameriken
American football

siklism
cycling

tenis
tennis

basketball
basketball

natasion
swimming

labox
boxing

oke lor gazon
ice hockey

foutborl
football

badminton
badminton

atletism
athletics

handball
handball

ski
skiing

polo
polo

aktivite

activities

riye
laugh
sote
jump
maye
hug
marse
walk
sante
sing
reve
dream
priye
pray
anbrase
kiss

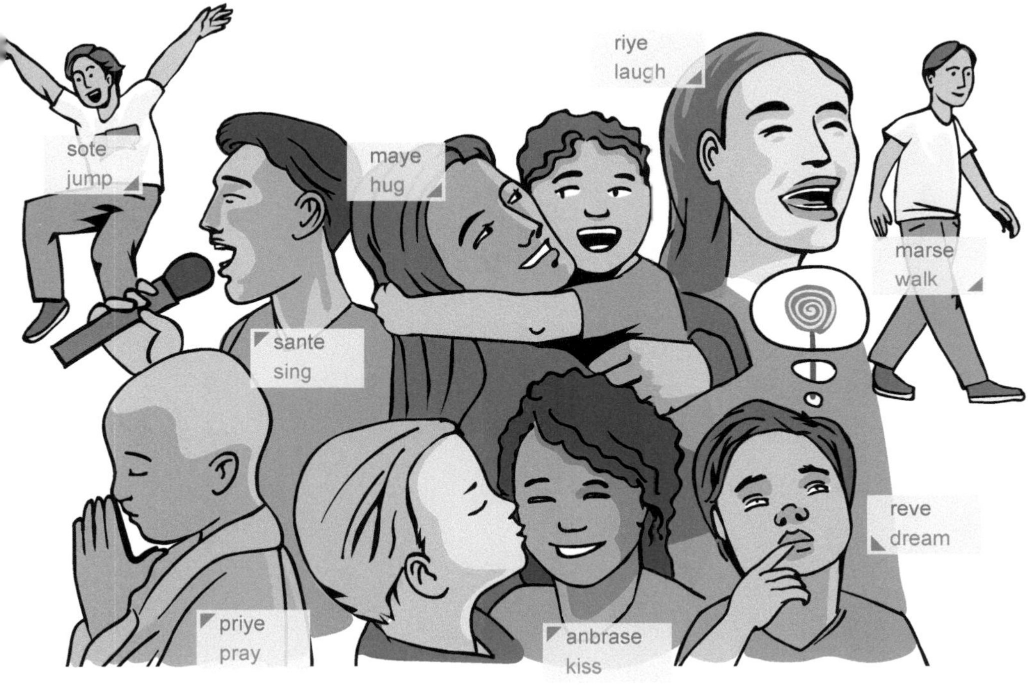

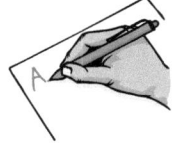

ekrir

write

desine

draw

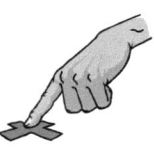

montre

show

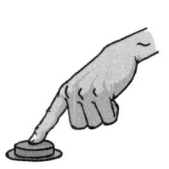

pouse

push

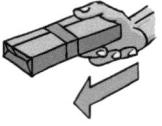

done

give

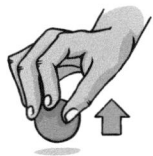

pran

take

ena
have

fer
do

ete
be

diboute
stand

galoupe
run

rise
pull

zete
throw

tonbe
fall

alonze
lie

atann
wait

amene
carry

asize
sit

abiye
get dressed

dormi
sleep

leve
wake up

gete

look at

plore

cry

karese

stroke

pengne

comb

koze

talk

konpran

understand

dimande

ask

ekoute

listen

bwar

drink

manze

eat

netwaye

tidy up

kontan

love

kwi

cook

kondir

drive

anvole

fly

aktivite - activities

fer lavwal
....
sail

kalkile
....
calculate

lir
....
read

aprann
....
learn

travay
....
work

marye
....
marry

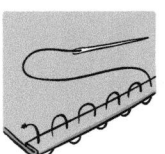

koud
....
sew

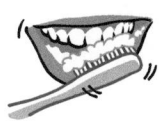

bros ledan
....
brush teeth

touye
....
kill

fime
....
smoke

avoye
....
send

fami

family

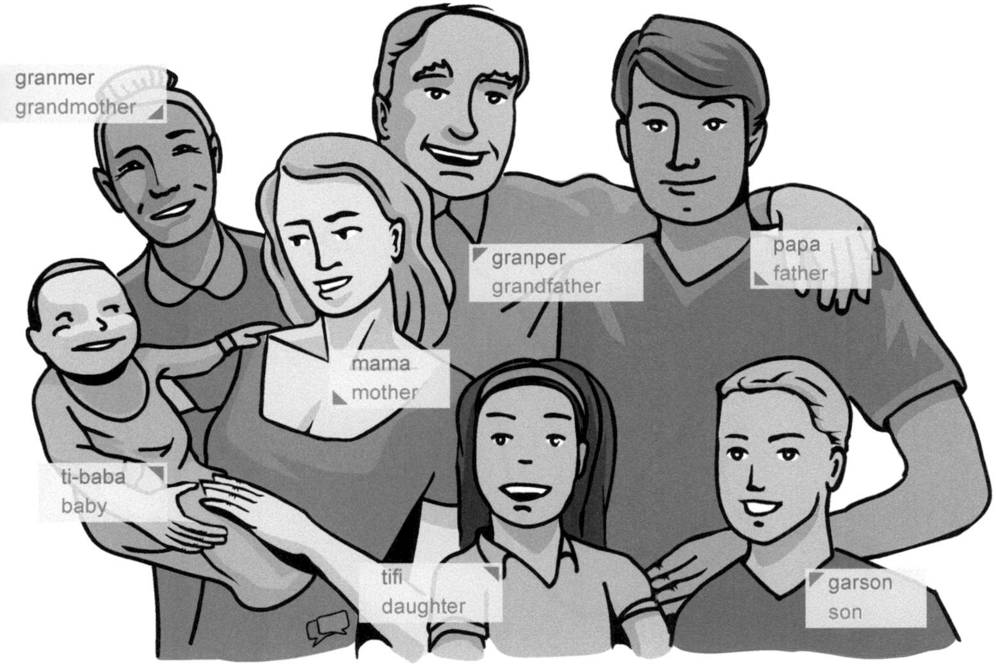
granmer
grandmother
granper
grandfather
papa
father
mama
mother
ti-baba
baby
tifi
daughter
garson
son

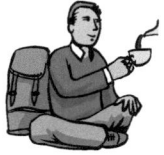

ot

guest

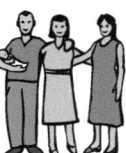

matant

aunt

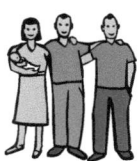

tonton

uncle

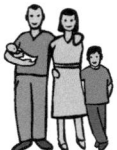

frer

brother

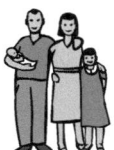

ser

sister

lekor

body

fron
forehead
lizie
eye
figir
face
manton
chin
tete
breast
ledwa
finger
lame
hand
lebra
arm
zepol
shoulder
lazam
leg

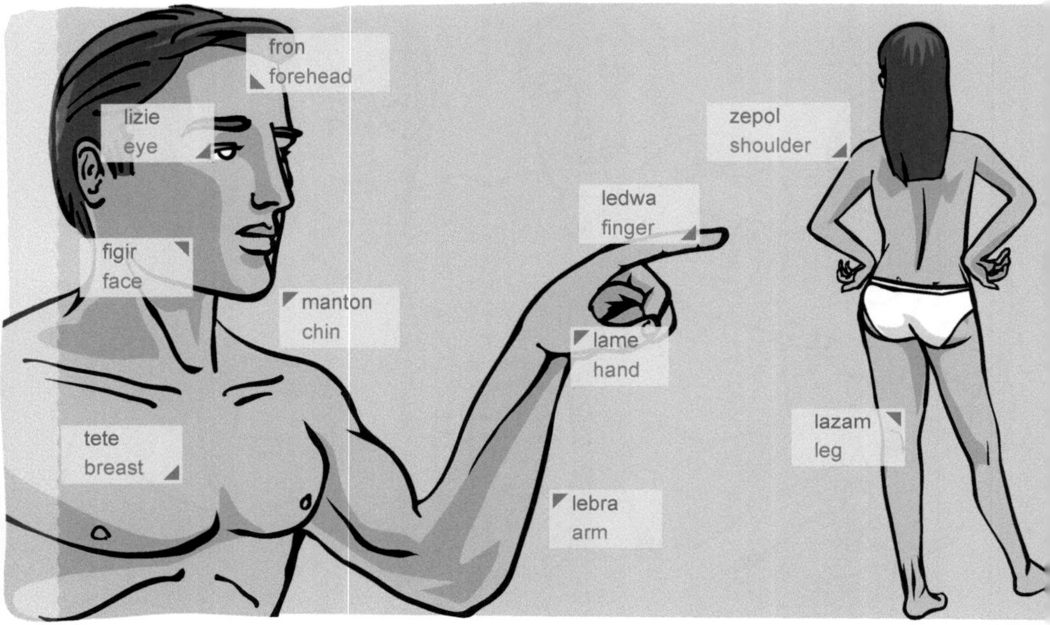

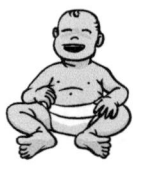

ti-baba

baby

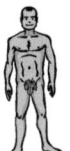

zom

man

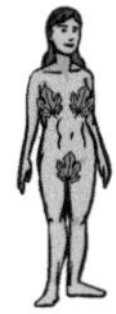

fam

woman

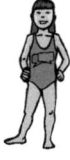

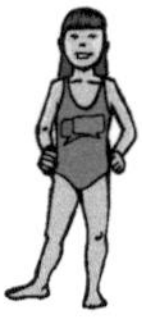

tifi

girl

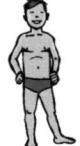

ti-garson

boy

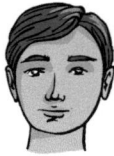

latet

head

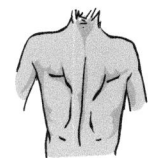

ledo

back

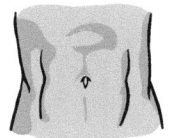

vant

belly

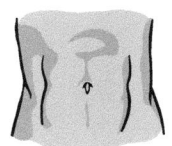

lonbri

belly button

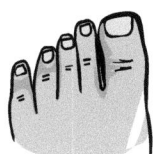

zortey

toe

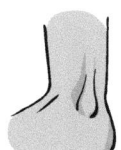

talon

heel

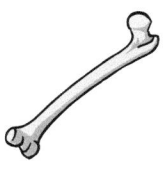

lezo

bone

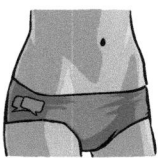

laans

hip

zenou

knee

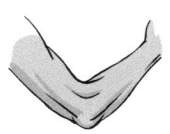

koud

elbow

nene

nose

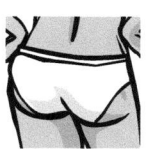

fes

bottom

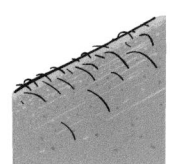

lapo

skin

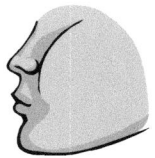

lazou

cheek

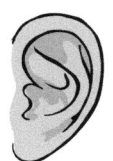

zorey

ear

lalev

lip

lekor - body

labous

mouth

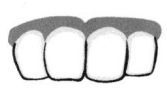

ledan

tooth

lalang

tongue

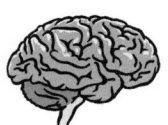

servo

brain

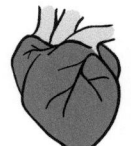

leker

heart

mix

muscle

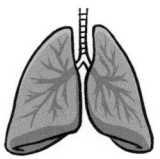

poumon

lung

lefwa

liver

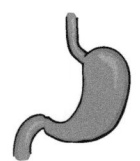

lestoma

stomach

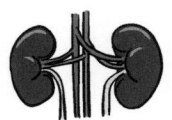

lerin

kidneys

sex

sex

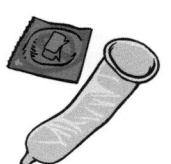

kapot

condom

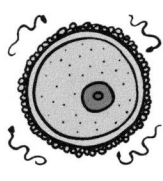

ovil

ovum

sperm

semen

groses

pregnancy

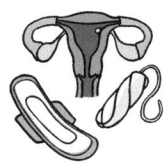

period
menstruation

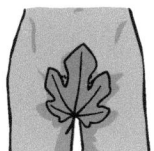

vazin
vagina

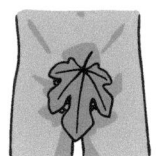

penis
penis

soursi
eyebrow

seve
hair

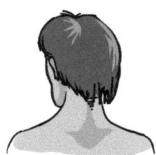

likou
neck

lopital
hospital

lopital
hospital
lanbilans
ambulance
fotey-roulan
wheelchair
fraktir
fracture

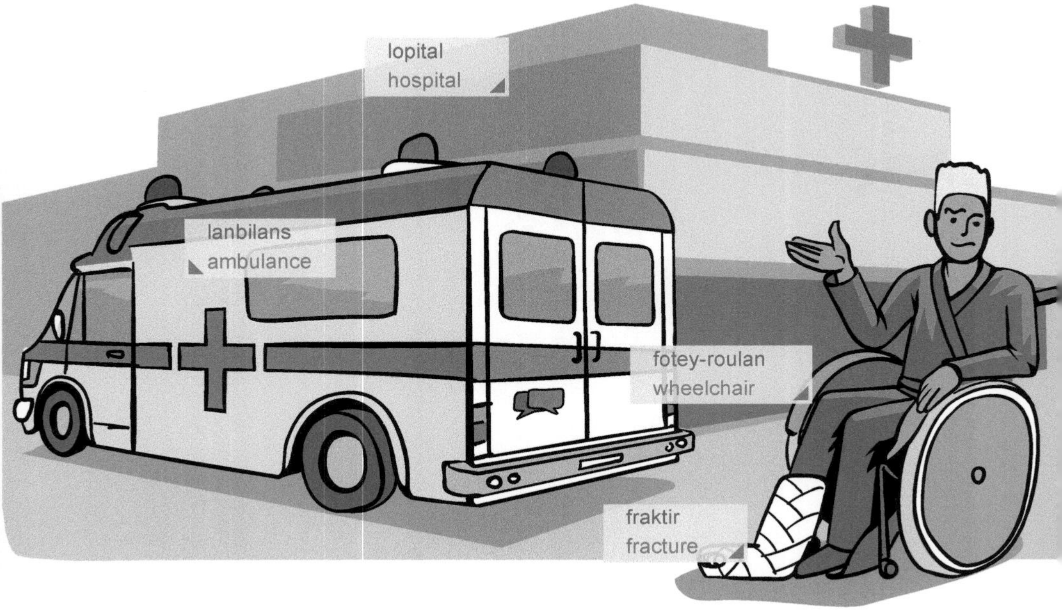

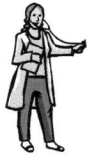

dokter

doctor

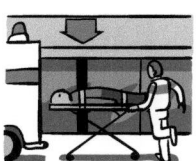

servis irzans

emergency room

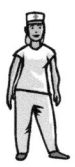

ners

nurse

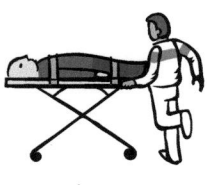

irzans

emergency

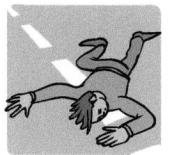

inkonsian

unconscious

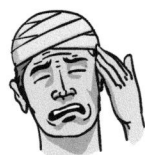

douler

pain

blesir
injury

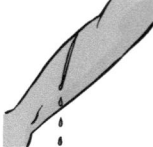

emorazi
bleeding

kriz kardiak
heart attack

atak serebral
stroke

alerzik
allergy

touse
cough

lafiev
fever

lagrip
flu

diare
diarrhoea

malad latet
headache

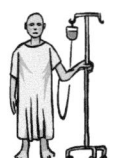

kanser
cancer

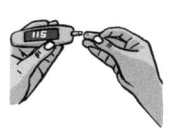

diabet
diabetes

sirirzien
surgeon

skalpel
scalpel

operasion
operation

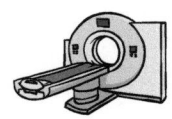

CT
CT

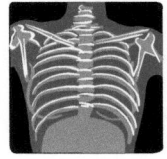

x-ray
x-ray

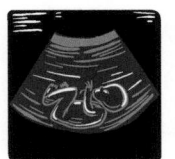

iltrason
ultrasound

mask
face mask

maladi
disease

sal-datant
waiting room

beki
crutch

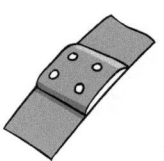

pansman
plaster

bandaz
bandage

inzeksion
injection

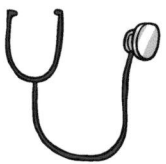

stetoskop
stethoscope

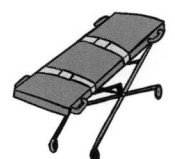

brankar
stretcher

termomet
clinical thermometer

nesans
birth

sirpwa
overweight

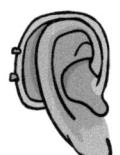

laparey oditif

hearing aid

dezinfektan

disinfectant

infeksion

infection

viris

virus

HIV / SIDA

HIV / AIDS

medsinn

medicine

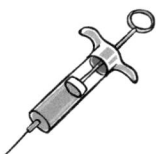

vaksinasion

vaccination

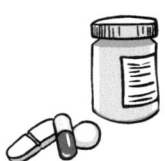

konprime

tablets

pilil kontraseptif

pill

korl irzans

emergency call

laparey tansion

blood pressure monitor

malad / bien

ill / healthy

o-sekour

Help!

alarm

alarm

atak

assault

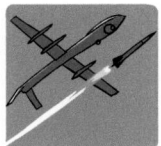

atak

attack

danze

danger

sorti de sekour

emergency exit

Dife!

Fire!

laponp dife

fire extinguisher

aksidan

accident

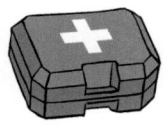

kit first aid

first-aid kit

SOS

SOS

lapolis

police

Ierop
....
Europe

Lamerik di nor
....
North America

Lamerik di sid
....
South America

Iafrik
....
Africa

Iazi
....
Asia

Iostrali
....
Australia

latlantik
....
Atlantic

pasifik
....
Pacific

Iosean indien
....
Indian Ocean

Iosean antartik
....
Antarctic Ocean

Iosean artik
....
Arctic Ocean

Pol Nor
....
North Pole

Pol Sid

South Pole

lantartik

Antarctica

later

Earth

later

land

lamer

sea

zil

island

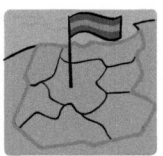

nasion

nation

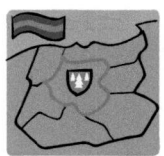

leta

state

kadran

clock face

zegwi ler

hour hand

zegwi minit

minute hand

zegwi segonn

second hand

ki ler la ?

What time is it?

zour

day

letan

time

aster-la

now

mont dizital

digital watch

minit

minute

ler

hour

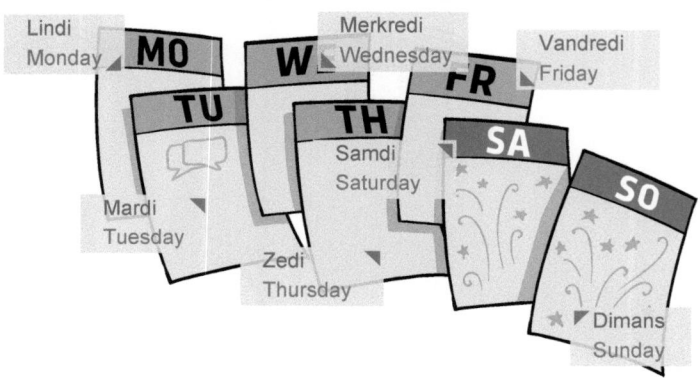

Lindi / Monday
Mardi / Tuesday
Merkredi / Wednesday
Zedi / Thursday
Vandredi / Friday
Samdi / Saturday
Dimans / Sunday

yer

yesterday

zordi

today

demin

tomorrow

gramatin

morning

midi

noon

aswar

evening

MO	TU	WE	TH	FR	SA	SU
1	2	3	4	5	6	7
8	9	10	11	12	13	14
15	16	17	18	19	20	21
22	23	24	25	26	27	28
29	30	31	1	2	3	4

zour travay

business days

MO	TU	WE	TH	FR	SA	SU
1	2	3	4	5	6	7
8	9	10	11	12	13	14
15	16	17	18	19	20	21
22	23	24	25	26	27	28
29	30	31	1	2	3	4

wikenn

weekend

lane
year

lapli
rain
larkansiel
rainbow
divan[
wind
lanez
snow
printan
spring
lete
summer
otonn
autumn
liver
winter

4.APRIL 11°
5.APRIL 4°
6.APRIL 13°
7.APRIL 8°
8.APRIL 10°

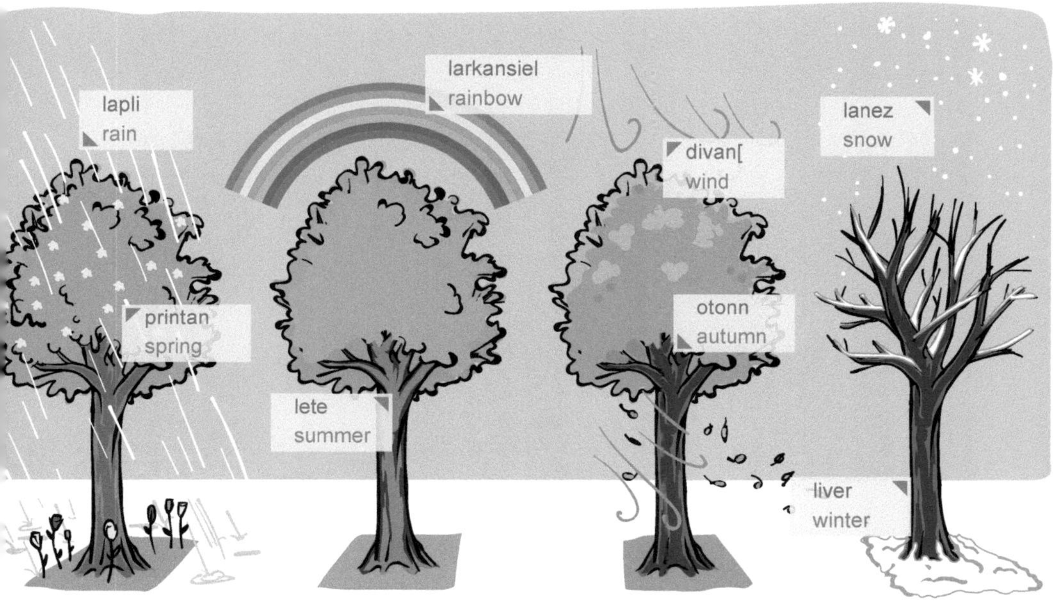

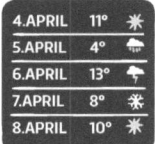

meteo

weather forecast

F C
120 40
90 30
60 20
30 10
0 0
-30 -10
-20

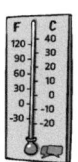

termomet

thermometer

lalimier soley

sunshine

niaz

cloud

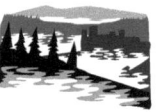

brouyar

fog

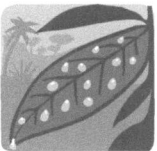

limidite

humidity

lafoud

lightning

toner

thunder

tanpet

storm

lagrel

hail

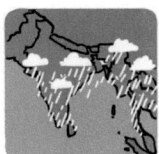

mouson

monsoon

inondasion

flood

laglas

ice

Zanvie

January

Fevriye

February

Mars

March

Avril

April

Me

May

Zien

June

Zilie

July

Out

August

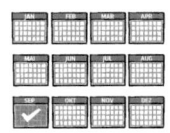

Septam
....
September

Oktob
....
October

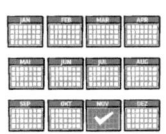

Novam
....
November

Desam
....
December

ron
....
circle

kare
....
square

rektang
....
rectangle

triang
....
triangle

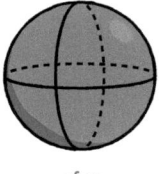

sfer
....
sphere

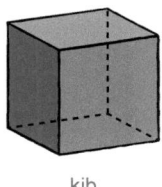

kib
....
cube

blan

white

zonn

yellow

oranz

orange

roz

pink

rouz

red

mov

purple

ble

blue

ver

green

maron

brown

gri

grey

nwar

black

boukou / enn tigit
a lot / a little

ankoler / kalm
angry / calm

zoli / vilin
beautiful / ugly

koumansman / lafin
beginning / end

gro / tipti
big / small

kler / obskirite
bright / dark

frer / ser
brother / sister

prop / sal
clean / dirty

konple / inkonple
complete / incomplete

lizour / lanwit
day / night

vivan / mor
dead / alive

larz / sere
wide / narrow

komestib / inkomestib

edible / inedible

move / bon

evil / kind

exsite / agase

excited / bored

gra / mins

fat / thin

premie / dernie

first / last

kamwad / lennmi

friend / enemy

ranpli / vid

full / empty

dir / mou

hard / soft

lour / leze

heavy / light

fin / swaf

hunger / thirst

malad / bien

ill / healthy

ilegal / legal

illegal / legal

intelizan / kouyon

intelligent / stupid

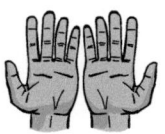

gos / drwat

left / right

pre / lwin

near / far

nouvo / ize

new / used

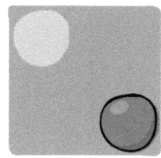

nanye / kiksoz

nothing / something

vie / zenn

old / young

demare / arete

on / off

ouver / ferme

open / closed

trankil / for

quiet / loud

ris / pov

rich / poor

bon / move

right / wrong

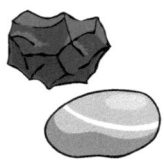

brit / lis

rough / smooth

tris / zwaye

sad / happy

kourt / long

short / long

lan / rapid

slow / fast

tranpe / sek

wet / dry

so / fre

warm / cool

lager / lape

war / peace

opozision - opposites

0

zero

zero

1

enn

one

2

de

two

3

trwa

three

4

kat

four

5

sink

five

6

sis

six

7

set

seven

8

wit

eight

9

nef

nine

10

distribiter biye

ten

11

onz

eleven

12

douz

twelve

13

trez

thirteen

14

katorz

fourteen

15

kinz

fifteen

16

sez

sixteen

17

diset

seventeen

18

dizwit

eighteen

19

diznef

nineteen

20

vin

twenty

100

san

hundred

1.000

mil

thousand

1.000.000

milyon

million

Angle

English

Angle Lamerik

American English

Mandarin Sinwa

Chinese Mandarin

Hindi

Hindi

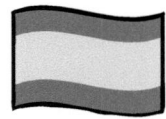

espagnol

Spanish

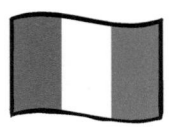

Franse

French

Arab

Arabic

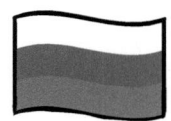

Ris

Russian

Portige

Portuguese

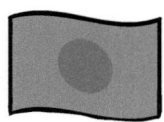

Bengali

Bengali

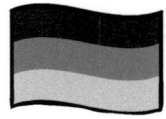

Alman

German

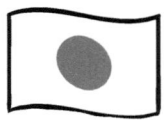

Zapone

Japanese

mo

I

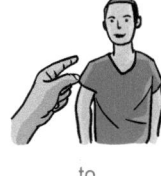

to

you

li

he / she / it

nou

we

ou

you

zot

they

kisana?

who?

kiete?

what?

kouma?

how?

kotsa?

where?

kan?

when?

nom

name

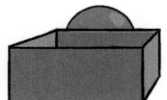

deryer

behind

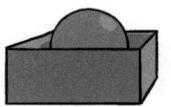

dan

in

devan

in front of

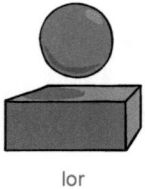

lor

over

lor

on

anba

under

akote

beside

ant

between

plas

place